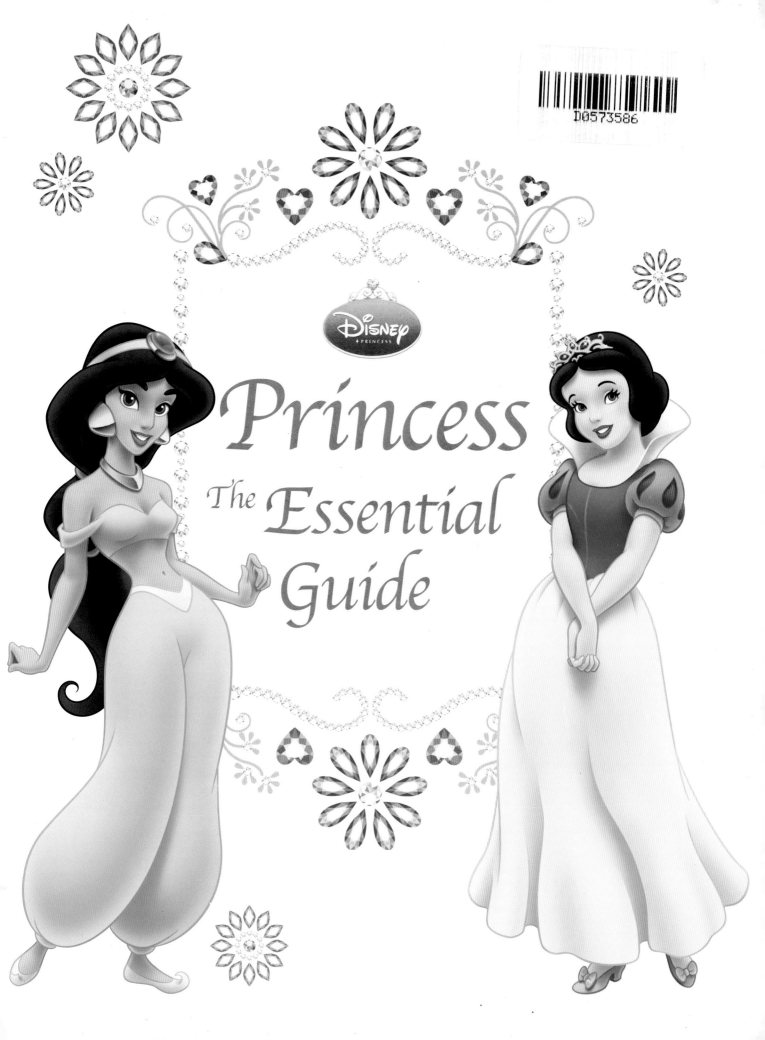

Disney
PRINCESS

Princess
The Essential Guide

We're together now.
Everything's going
to be fine, you'll see.

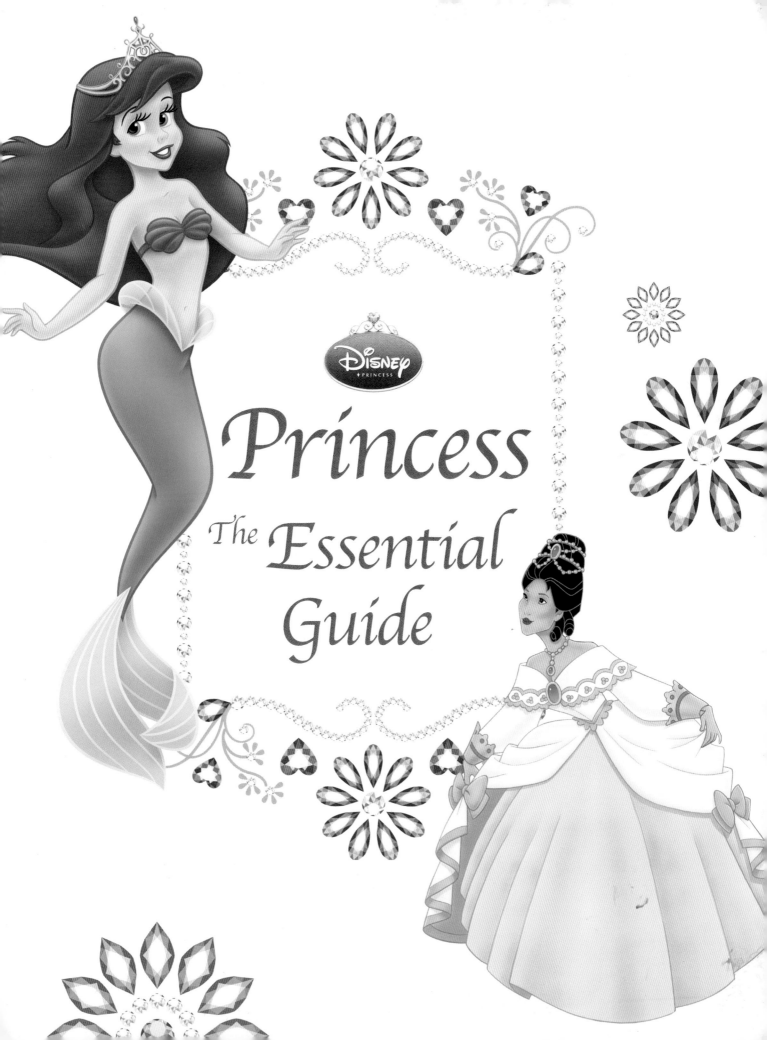

Princess

The Essential Guide

Contents

*If you keep on believing,
the dreams that you wish
will come true.*

Introduction

Snow White

Aurora

Cinderella

Ariel

BY ROYAL DECREE you are cordially invited to visit some far-off lands and meet some fabulous princesses. Be prepared for tales of magic spells, amazing courage, special friendships, and, of course, true love. You will discover that being a princess is not just about wearing beautiful dresses and falling in love with handsome princes—although that is the fun part!

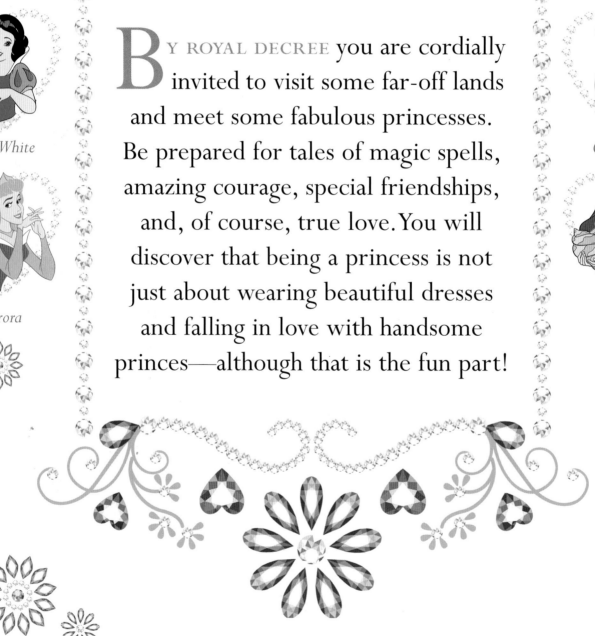

Belle

Jasmine

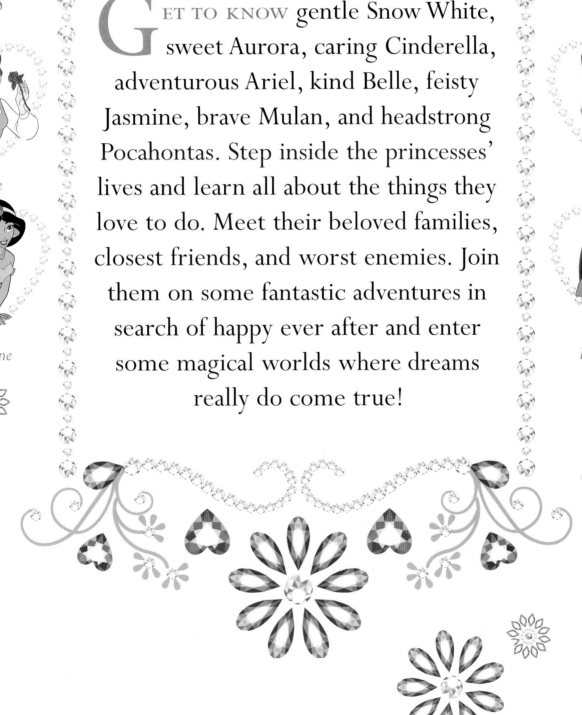

G ET TO KNOW gentle Snow White, sweet Aurora, caring Cinderella, adventurous Ariel, kind Belle, feisty Jasmine, brave Mulan, and headstrong Pocahontas. Step inside the princesses' lives and learn all about the things they love to do. Meet their beloved families, closest friends, and worst enemies. Join them on some fantastic adventures in search of happy ever after and enter some magical worlds where dreams really do come true!

Mulan

Pocahontas

Snow White

*O*nce upon a time in a magical land
there lived a beautiful young princess
with hair as black as ebony, lips as red as
roses and skin as white as snow. Her name
was Snow White. Everyone loved Snow White,
apart from her wicked stepmother, the Queen,
who was jealous of Snow White's beauty.

Some day my prince will come.

Princess in peril

THE QUEEN FEARS that Snow White will grow more beautiful than her, so she treats her like a servant. When the Magic Mirror reveals that Snow White has become fairer than her wicked stepmother, her life is in danger—until she finds seven little friends to help her!

Her favorite things

Singing and dancing always cheer Snow White up, and give her courage when she's afraid.

Telling stories is one of Snow White's great talents. The Seven Dwarfs like to listen to her stories about the day her prince will come and how they will live happily in a beautiful castle.

The animals and birds of the forest love Snow White's kind and gentle nature. They even help her clean up the Dwarfs' messy cottage!

Her hair is as black as ebony.

Her lips are as red as roses.

The lining of her sleeves match her hair ribbon.

ABOUT SNOW WHITE

♥ She's so sweet and gentle, she makes lots of friends wherever she goes.

♥ She is always cheerful and looks on the bright side.

♥ She is romantic and longs to meet her true love.

♥ She is practical and works hard.

Snow White loves to walk in the Enchanted Forest and pick the pretty flowers. But she can't bring too many into the cottage because flowers make Sneezy sneeze!

Snow White sews her own petticoats to wear underneath her dresses.

When the Dwarfs find out that Snow White is a good cook, they are delighted. Even more so when they discover she can bake their favorite gooseberry pie!

Oh, it's adorable!

✖ *Love and romance*

It seems like Snow White's wish for love will never come true, spending all her time working hard for the Queen.

But love always finds a way and even in her tattered rags, the Prince is captivated by Snow White's beauty.

11

Snow White's world

SNOW WHITE LIVES IN AN ENCHANTED land with seven jeweled hills and seven waterfalls. Beyond the farthest hill stands the castle where she grew up with her wicked stepmother, the Queen. From here you can see the pretty little cottage where the Seven Dwarfs live.

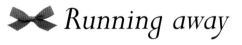 *Running away*

In the Dark Forest, even the trees seem to be against Snow White as she runs away from the Queen.

Snow White has nowhere to go and gets lost in the dense forest. Eventually she can run no farther and she falls to the ground in tears.

In disguise, the Queen sets off by boat to find Snow White.

The Queen's laboratory and dungeons lie below the castle.

The clearing where Snow White meets the friendly forest animals

❧ The Prince

More than anything, Snow White longs for her Prince to carry her away to his castle, where they will live happily ever after.

The seven hills really are jeweled because there are dazzling diamonds inside. The Seven Dwarfs love to dig, dig, dig all day long in the mines.

The Prince's castle

The evil Queen tries to use the rock to stop the Dwarfs.

Entrance to the mines

The Enchanted Forest where Snow White sleeps in a glass coffin.

❧ The cottage

The Seven Dwarfs are not very good at keeping their home clean and tidy! Snow White hopes to surprise them and cleans the cottage with some help from her little animal friends.

The Dwarfs' cottage

13

Friends and enemies

ONE OF THE GREAT GIFTS Snow White has is the ability to make friends easily; the animals and Dwarfs would do anything for her. Even Grumpy! But the Queen is madly jealous of her naturally beautiful stepdaughter. And the cruel Queen is a very dangerous enemy to have.

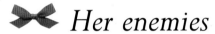 ## Her enemies

As well as being Snow White's stepmother, the Queen is also a wicked witch. She hates Snow White so much that she uses a poisoned apple to try and get rid of her.

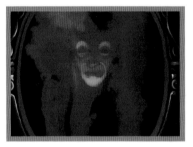

'Magic Mirror on the wall, who is the fairest one of all?'

The Magic Mirror must answer all the questions that the jealous Queen asks.

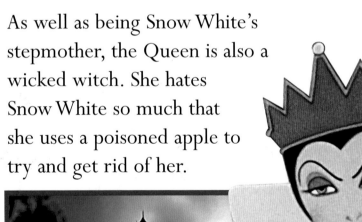

Despite being pure evil, the Queen has a cold beauty.

The poisoned apple

Before turning red, for a moment the apple reveals the poison that covers it.

Although the Huntsman is a loyal servant of the Queen, he is not really wicked. Seeing Snow White's sweet nature, he cannot bear to carry out the Queen's order to kill the innocent princess.

❀ *Her friends*

The Seven Dwarfs and the birds and animals that meet Snow White love

her dearly. They try to protect her from the wicked Queen and her evil spells.

Grumpy Doc Bashful Sneezy Happy Dopey Sleepy

A wish comes true

FROM THE MOMENT THAT SNOW WHITE becomes more beautiful than the Queen, her life is in danger. Although the Seven Dwarfs try their best, they cannot protect her from the Queen's black magic. But good is stronger than evil, and in the end the Prince's love for Snow White saves the day.

✖ One spring morning

Snow White sings while she cleans. The Prince hears her and falls in love.

I beg of you, your Highness, forgive me!

The Magic Mirror tells the Queen that Snow White is the fairest in the land. The Queen orders the Huntsman to take the princess out to pick flowers in the forest and kill her.

Although he tries, the Huntsman can't bring himself to harm her and tells Snow White to run away. She flees and hides in the little cottage in the forest.

The cottage is owned by the Seven Dwarfs. When they come home to find a stranger in their home, they are afraid. But as soon as they meet Snow White, they want her to stay with them forever.

The poisoned apple

Disguised as an ugly old peddler woman, the Queen persuades trusting Snow White to take one bite of the poisoned apple. She promises this will make all her dreams come true.

No harm can come to Snow White now that her Prince has come.

There's nobody like him anywhere at all.

As soon as Snow White takes a bite of the apple, she falls to the ground in a deep sleep and cannot be woken. When the Dwarfs find her they place her in a special glass coffin, and keep a vigil at her side.

The Prince finds Snow White in the forest and wakes her from her slumber with true love's kiss. They set off for his palace and a future filled with happiness.

Cinderella

*O*nce upon a time a young girl lived happily with her father, stepmother, and stepsisters. One sad day the girl's father died, leaving her stepmother in charge. Before she knew it, the girl was forced to work as a servant to her stepmother and stepsisters. She became known as Cinderella.

Why, it's like a dream.
A wonderful dream
come true.

Servant girl

FROM THE MOMENT HER BELOVED FATHER dies, Cinderella's life changes forever. Her cruel Stepmother and spoiled stepsisters make her life miserable, but she never stops hoping and believing that one day her life will change and a handsome prince will sweep her off her feet.

Her friends

Although they are only tiny mice, Gus and Jaq are Cinderella's loyal friends. They help with her chores and save her from being lonely.

ABOUT CINDERELLA

♥ She is cheerful and sunny, no matter how difficult things are.

♥ Cinderella is hard-working and practical and can cook and sew.

♥ She is very caring, and her heart is full of kindness.

Delicate lace petticoat

The Fairy Godmother makes Cinderella's dreams of happiness come true. Her magic spell makes it possible for Cinderella to go to the ball, even if it is only for a few hours.

The long, flowing skirt, made of shimmering sky-blue satin, reflects the color of her eyes.

Headband matches gown

Puffy sleeves

Elegant evening gloves

Her clothes

Cinderella has no money to spend on clothes. Her animal friends help to patch up her simple dress and apron each morning and shine her worn-out shoes.

The birds and mice sew frills and bows on an old dress that once belonged to her mother, so that Cinderella can go to the ball.

If you tell a wish it won't come true!

Cinderella marries Prince Charming, wearing a beautiful dress of white silk with a long train.

21

Home sweet home

Cinderella's tiny attic bedroom

ONCE UPON A TIME, the manor house was the happiest place in the whole of the kingdom. But when Cinderella's mean Stepmother arrives, things change. Lady Tremaine makes Cinderella sleep in the attic and do household chores all day long.

While her father is alive, the house is happy.

Home life

Cinderella can see the beautiful castle from her bedroom window, and she imagines how wonderful it would be to live there.

Every morning Cinderella feeds the animals before she takes breakfast up to her Stepmother, in bed.

The kitchen where Cinderella spends much of her day cooking and cleaning

Door to courtyard

Mouse hole

Family and friends

Jaq and Gus care deeply for Cinderella. The same cannot be said for her family; she waits on them hand and foot without any thanks!

Lady Tremaine and her spoiled daughters, Drizella and Anastasia, hate Cinderella because of her natural beauty.

Doors to Drizella and Anastasia's grand bedrooms

Lady Tremaine's bedroom is three times bigger than Cinderella's attic room.

Lucifer's velvet bed

Lucifer the cat lies in wait for the mice to torment them. Even Cinderella, who loves most animals, hasn't a good word to say about him!

Music room

Magic moments

A LITTLE MAGIC IS ALL Cinderella needs to find happiness after her father dies. She has charm and beauty, and all the elegance of a princess, and with a little help from her Fairy Godmother her dreams come true.

The invitation

To celebrate the Prince's return, all eligible ladies in the land are invited to attend a ball at the castle.

Cinderella's ugly stepsisters cannot bear to see her looking so beautiful in her mother's dress. They are so jealous they tear her outfit to pieces.

With a wave of her magic wand, the Fairy Godmother ensures that Cinderella can go to the ball.

🥿 The ball

As soon as their eyes meet at the ball, Cinderella and the Prince fall in love. But when the clock strikes twelve, Cinderella leaves her glass slipper behind on the stairs in her hurry to leave before the magic ends. Soon her dress turns into rags.

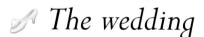

Cinderella's golden hair is swept up on her head and she looks like a real princess.

The Grand Duke is absolutely delighted when Cinderella produces the matching glass slipper and slips it on to her dainty foot. Lady Tremaine, on the other hand, is furious.

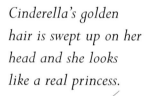

Magic is in the air!

🥿 The wedding

After all his searching, Prince Charming has at last found the beautiful girl he danced with at the ball. The whole kingdom rejoices when he marries Cinderella.

Sleeping Beauty

*I*n a far away land there lived a king and queen who longed to have a child. After many years their wish was granted with the birth of a daughter who they named Aurora. When an evil fairy placed a curse on the young princess, her parents sent her to live with the good fairies in the woods. The fairies re-named the girl Briar Rose.

Well, I'm really not supposed to speak to strangers, but we've met before.

Hidden princess

BROUGHT UP IN THE COUNTRYSIDE, this sweet and gentle girl has no idea that she is really a princess named Aurora. She learns the truth on her sixteenth birthday, the same day that, due to a curse put on her by a wicked fairy, she falls into an enchanted sleep. Only true love's first kiss saves her from eternal slumber.

ABOUT AURORA

♥ She's gentle and sweet-natured. All who know her love her.
♥ Aurora is thoughtful and unspoiled. She is always willing to help.
♥ She is a romantic and believes that her dreams of love will one day come true.

Her favorite things

As a baby, Aurora was given the gift of song. Her voice is sweet and pure, and she loves to sing to the animals in the forest.

Aurora lives in a cottage situated in the heart of a beautiful forest. The woods are her playground where she can think and dream, dip her toes in the stream, and pick sweet berries.

It takes lots of magic to create this beautiful dress, fit for a very special princess.

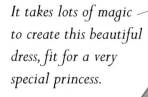

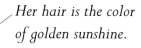

Her hair is the color of golden sunshine.

She is always ready with a smile.

Her beauty is as natural as a rose in bloom.

Her clothes

Growing up in the forest, Aurora has a simple wardrobe, but she is so unspoiled that she doesn't mind. And she is so beautiful that she looks lovely even in the plainest of dresses with just a shawl to wrap around her shoulders.

If you dream a thing more than once, it's sure to come true!

 The good fairies use their magic to make Aurora a stunning birthday dress. But should it be pink or blue? They just can't decide on the color!

Her princess dress

When Aurora wears the magical dress and her golden crown, she is transformed from a sheltered young girl into an elegant princess. Now she is ready to marry Prince Phillip and become a beautiful bride.

29

Forest life

THE GOOD FAIRIES TAKE BABY AURORA to live in a pretty little cottage, deep in the forest, to hide her from the wicked fairy's curse. They rename her Briar Rose after the wild flower that grows in the forest, and they live here happily for sixteen years.

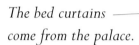

The bed curtains come from the palace.

Birthday celebrations

Unlike most princesses, who have servants, Briar Rose begins her birthday by helping her aunts to dust and spring-clean their little cottage!

The little birds love to visit Briar Rose in her bedroom.

Flora, Fauna, and Merryweather love Briar Rose dearly and have special plans for her birthday. They ask her to pick berries in the forest so that they can make her a surprize gift.

The sound of trickling water lulls Briar Rose to sleep at night.

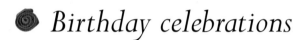

Briar Rose meets the man of her dreams in the forest and her birthday is the happiest ever. She doesn't realize that the handsome young man is actually a prince.

Sparks of blue and
pink magic escape
from the chimney.

The roof is
made of straw.

Fauna

Flora

Merryweather

The chamber where Aurora sleeps peacefully

Her bed is draped in rich velvet.

The spiral staircase leads to the secret chamber.

Castle life

NAMED AURORA AFTER THE DAWN because like a new day, she brought sunshine into her proud parents' lives, the baby princess seemed to have all she could wish for. But not for long! At the party given to celebrate her birth, the wicked fairy, Maleficent, promised that Aurora would prick her finger on a spindle and die before the sun set on her sixteenth birthday.

Baby celebrations

Flora and Fauna bless Aurora with gifts of song and beauty. But Merryweather still has her gift to give when Maleficent arrives.

At the party, King Hubert and King Stefan celebrate the betrothal of their children, Phillip and Aurora.

The good fairies rush to try and save Aurora.

The fire dies down to reveal a secret door to the tower.

Prince Phillip is the only one who can wake Aurora.

Maleficent is very offended when she is not invited to the royal party. She is so angry that she curses the baby Aurora. But luckily Merryweather has one gift to give and lessens the curse.

Sixteen years later

Maleficent's curse comes true when Aurora pricks her finger on a spinning wheel and falls into a deep sleep. When Prince Phillip tries to save Aurora, Maleficent turns into a fierce dragon—but with the Sword of Truth and Shield of Virtue he defeats her.

Sleeping Beauty

AS FAR AS AURORA IS CONCERNED, her life has been uneventful. For sixteen years she has lived in the forest longing for excitement and romance, with no friends other than the woodland animals. Then, on her sixteenth birthday, everything seems to happen at once!

The early years

Aurora's life changes forever when Maleficent arrives at the royal party and casts her evil spell.

Briar Rose meets Phillip whilst picking berries in the forest. The handsome young prince is the man of her dreams and they fall head-over-heels in love with each other.

Briar Rose is upset when the fairies tell her that she is a princess. She doesn't want to marry a prince she has never met! She doesn't realize that the prince she is to marry is the man she loves.

🌹 *Her birthday*

As soon as Aurora pricks her finger on the spindle, she feels dizzy and sinks into a deep sleep.

We've met before.

Once upon a dream!

When the fairies find Aurora asleep, they know that the King and Queen will be heartbroken.

Prince Phillip can't take his eyes off the beautiful princess.

The precious golden crown is a present from the good fairies.

The floaty skirt makes her feel like she's dancing on air.

When Phillip kisses Aurora, Maleficent's curse is broken and she wakes from her sleep.

35

Ariel

*D*eep under the ocean in a beautiful watery kingdom there lived a little mermaid, named Princess Ariel. She was the youngest daughter of Triton, the Sea King and full of curiosity about the world outside the ocean. Ariel's greatest wish was to live like a human on dry land.

Daddy, I love him!

Unhappy princess

Princess Ariel is a beautiful mermaid. She loves her father and older sisters, but she is not happy with her life underwater. She is determined to realize her dream of being a human on dry land, especially when she sets eyes upon handsome Prince Eric. Young and headstrong, Ariel usually gets her own way, but there is a price to pay.

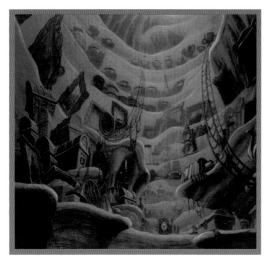

Ariel loves to collect human objects she finds on sunken ships and the ocean floor. She stores her collection of treasures in a secret underwater grotto, close to the palace.

Her favorite things

Ariel's best friend is a little fish named Flounder. They go on many exciting adventures together and often end up in lots of trouble!

Sebastian is Triton's loyal crab composer and is supposed to watch over Ariel. He tries hard but finds it difficult to keep up with her!

Ariel consults her funny seagull friend, Scuttle, about all human things. He claims to be an expert!

A telescope makes a good hat!

Her fins help her to swim fast.

Exploring

Even if it means swimming into dangerous, shark-infested waters, Ariel cannot resist the temptation to explore the ocean for shipwrecks so that she can add to her amazing collection of human things.

King Triton cannot understand his youngest daughter's love for humans. He thinks that they are dangerous and forbids her to go exploring.

Her eyes are as blue as the ocean.

Seashell bikini top

Ariel's hair is the color of red sea anemones and floats in the water.

The tiny scales on her tail shimmer like sequins.

I don't see how a world that makes such wonderful things could be bad!

About Ariel

♥ She's adventurous and curious.
♥ Headstrong and impulsive, Ariel refuses to listen to her father.
♥ She is romantic and gives up her voice for love.
♥ Ariel is funny and brave.

39

Under the sea

DEEP UNDER THE OCEAN is a marvelous world of brightly-colored fish, corals and seaweeds, and a sparkling palace that is home to King Triton and his mermaid daughters. But danger lurks underwater too, if only Ariel would listen.

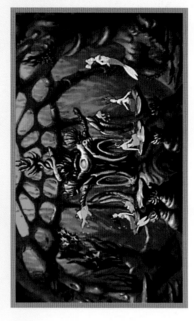

King Triton loves Ariel dearly and is prepared to give up everything he has to save her from Ursula, the sea witch.

The underwater palace

Ariel and her sisters' bedroom

King Triton's magnificent throne room

Ariel shares her bedroom with her six older sisters named Aquata, Andrina, Arista, Attina, Adella, and Alana. Sometimes Ariel finds it hard to be the youngest because everyone treats her like a child!

Treasures of the deep

Ariel is fascinated by all things from the human world, but she knows her father will be angry if he finds out about her secret collection.

She loves to examine the many objects in her cave and imagines what each thing is for.

Arches and tunnels are made from sea coral.

Giant clam shells make wonderful instruments in the concert hall.

Ursula

Ursula hates King Triton. The octopus-like sea witch longs to overthrow him so that she can become Queen of the Sea.

Ursula's spies, Flotsam and Jetsam, discover that Ariel is in love with Prince Eric and tell the sea witch. Ursula uses this to her advantage and offers Ariel a cruel deal.

On dry land

URSULA USES HER MAGIC TO MAKE ARIEL HUMAN and in exchange, Ariel gives up her beautiful voice. To stay human, Ariel must make Eric give her a kiss of true love within three days. If she fails, she will belong to Ursula. But Ariel doesn't realize that Ursula is up to no good and plans to use Ariel's voice to make Eric marry her! Luckily for Ariel, her friends and her father save the day.

★ Prince Eric

Ariel sees Prince Eric for the first time as his magnificent ship sails past. It is the prince's birthday and the crew celebrates with fireworks.

A violent storm throws the prince overboard but Ariel rescues him and takes him to the shore. She falls deeply in love with Eric but cannot survive on land for long and quickly returns to the sea.

As soon as Ariel drinks Ursula's magic potion, her tail disappears and in its place are two legs. It takes Scuttle a while to work out what's different about her!

Ariel loves being able to walk through the town square, and enjoys talking to all the people.

In the castle kitchen, the chef is determined to catch Sebastian and serve him up for dinner!

Without a voice, it is difficult for Ariel to get the prince to fall in love with her and kiss her.

Ariel's bedroom

The town

Roof-garden

Eric's ship

The sea view from the dining room means Ariel is never far from home.

When King Triton sees how much Ariel and Prince Eric love each other, he allows them to get married.

Belle

A long time ago in France, a beggar woman asked a handsome prince for shelter from the cold, in return for a single rose. The selfish prince refused to help and the old woman (who was really an enchantress) turned him into a hideous Beast. The spell would only be broken if the prince learned to truly love another person.

You have my word.

A sweet girl

BELLE, WHOSE NAME MEANS BEAUTY IN FRENCH, knows that true beauty lies within. But even her goodness is tested when she first sets eyes on the hideous-looking beast who lives in the enchanted castle. Although she doesn't know it, Belle's loving nature and intelligence have the power to transform the Beast into a handsome prince who will make her his princess bride.

ABOUT BELLE
- She is loyal and gives up her freedom for the father she adores.
- She's clever and makes her own judgments.
- She is imaginative and loves to read stories.

I've just finished a wonderful story!

✷ Village friends

Belle's only true friends in the village are the heroes and heroines she meets in the books she loves to read.

Although some people in the village think that Maurice is just a crazy old man, Belle has total faith in her father.

Dancing in this stunning gown, she is truly Belle of the ball.

Her long silky hair is the color of chocolate.

Her big brown eyes are full of warmth.

The rose is a symbol of Belle's love for the Beast.

✳ Castle friends

Lumiere and Cogsworth are two of the castle servants who are changed into household objects by the enchantress. They hope Belle will help them turn back into humans again.

Mrs. Potts, the kindly cook, and Chip, her playful son, cheer Belle up when she first arrives. They think that Belle is just the kind of girl to look beyond first appearances.

✳ Special clothes

At the castle, the Wardrobe provides Belle with all the clothes she could possibly want.

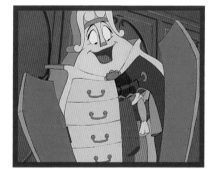

Belle loves the beautiful fur-lined cloak that the Wardrobe gives her. She wears the cloak when she goes walking with the Beast in the beautiful snowy gardens. They have lots of fun playing in the snow and Belle realizes how nice the Beast really is.

Belle's world

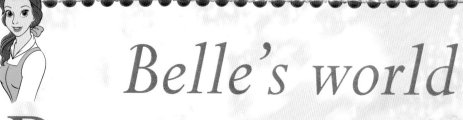

BELLE LIVES WITH HER father in a quiet little town where nothing ever happens, and she longs for adventure and a little romance. She soon discovers that not far away lies an enchanted castle and a very different world.

The head of the lunatic asylum calls to take Maurice away.

Belle's house is on the outskirts of town, making her an outsider in more ways than one.

❋ Gaston's admirers

No matter how hard they try, the three village girls cannot get Gaston to notice them. He only has eyes for the beautiful Belle.

The other girls in the village are not as pretty as Belle.

With her nose in a book all day long, Belle hardly notices the things that go on in the town around her. She dreams of a different life far, far away.

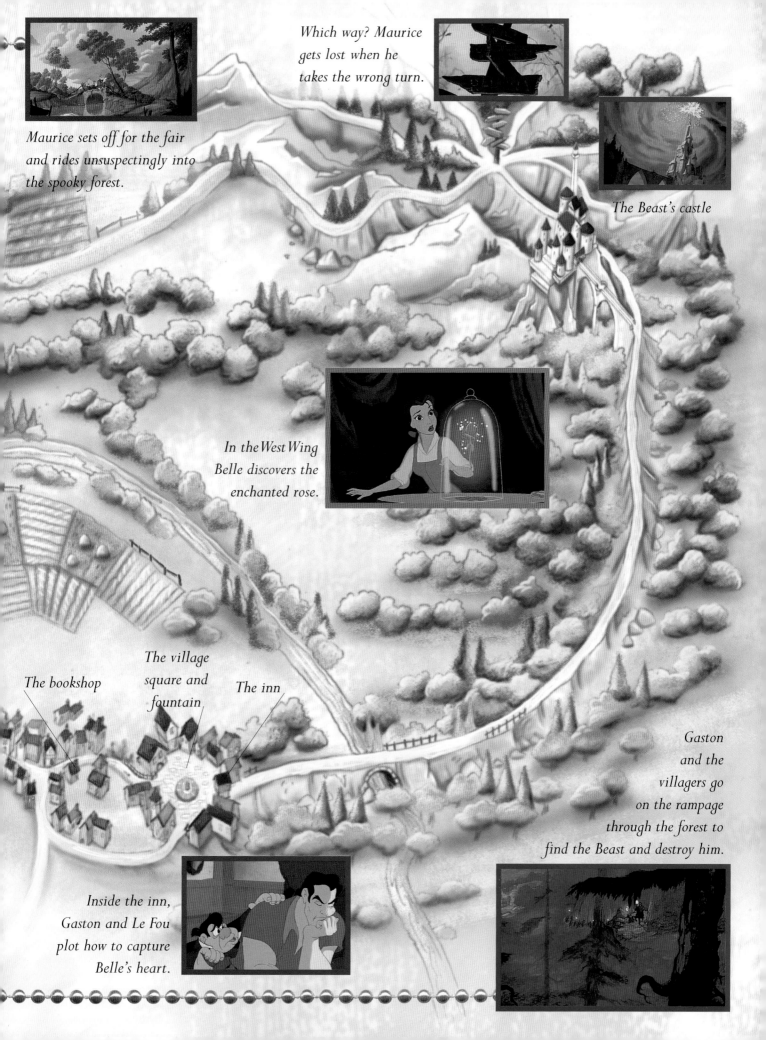

Maurice sets off for the fair and rides unsuspectingly into the spooky forest.

Which way? Maurice gets lost when he takes the wrong turn.

The Beast's castle

In the West Wing Belle discovers the enchanted rose.

The bookshop

The village square and fountain

The inn

Gaston and the villagers go on the rampage through the forest to find the Beast and destroy him.

Inside the inn, Gaston and Le Fou plot how to capture Belle's heart.

Learning to love

AT FIRST, BELLE IS DESPERATELY UNHAPPY at being imprisoned in the castle, but soon learns to love the enchanted objects. Taming the bad-tempered Beast takes longer and what she doesn't know is that time is running out. The Beast must learn to love and be loved before the last petal of the enchanted rose falls or he will remain a Beast forever.

Gaston and the Beast

Gaston may be handsome to look at, but when he proposes Belle is horrified at the thought of marrying such a vain and stupid man.

Belle loves her father so much that, although scared, she promises to stay in the Beast's castle forever so her father can be free.

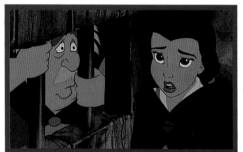

Belle is a beauty by nature as well as by name.

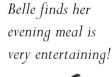

Belle finds her evening meal is very entertaining!

The magical servants are overjoyed to welcome Belle to the enchanted castle. She is the first guest they have had for years!

His true nature

When the Beast learns to control his temper, Belle sees the kind and loving person within.

The Beast grants Belle her freedom so that she can help her father. This is a sign of his true love for her because he is willing to give up his only chance of becoming human again. This act of kindness makes Belle realize how much she loves him.

Belle manages to uncover the Beast's true nature.

The transformation

The Beast is terribly wounded by Gaston and Belle fears she is too late to save him. Tearfully she confesses her love for him and the spell is broken. The Beast regains his appearance as a handsome prince and all the enchanted objects become humans again.

Belle loves the Beast no matter what he looks like.

Jasmine

B rought up in a life of luxury in a far-off land, Princess Jasmine longed for adventure and excitement and the freedom to make her own choices. The last thing she wanted was to marry a silly, dull prince as the law and her father, the Sultan, said she must.

I am not a prize to be won!

Eastern princess

A sparkling sapphire is fixed upon her headband.

Princess Jasmine cannot bear being a princess. It's so boring! When she meets a street urchin named Aladdin, her life changes forever and she knows for sure that she could only marry someone she loves. Although her father and the evil Jafar have other plans for her, feisty Jasmine is not about to let them rule her life!

Her long, flowing hair is as smooth as satin.

♥ Likes

Jasmine's father is the Sultan of Agrabah and wants only the best for his daughter, including a prince for a husband.

She loves to wear her beautiful pink silk pants.

At first Abu is rude to Jasmine but she soon becomes very fond of the cheeky monkey.

Her chiffon wrap shimmers in the light.

Rajah is Jasmine's pet tiger and her closest friend in the palace. She tells him all her secrets and dreams.

Her slippers are made of gold.

54

💜 Dislikes

ABOUT JASMINE

💜 Fiercely independent—she longs to be free and able to make her own choices.

💜 She's brave and isn't afraid to stand up to Jafar and speak her own mind!

💜 She's adventurous and intelligent.

Jafar, the evil vizier and assistant to Jasmine's father, will never win her affection, no matter how powerful he is.

If I do marry I want it to be for love.

Jasmine hates not being free to go where she chooses. She decides to see for herself what life is like on the other side of the palace walls.

Jasmine is not impressed when her father introduces her to Prince Ali because she doesn't recognize Aladdin in his princely clothes. Jasmine is determined to choose her own husband.

Aladdin may be poor, but to Jasmine he is a prince.

Agrabah

JASMINE LIVES IN THE DESERT CITY

J of Agrabah, in a splendid palace with her father. It is a wonderful city of mystery and enchantment, but she has never been outside the palace walls. Jasmine longs to experience the noise and excitement of the lively city for herself.

Hold on tight for a bird's eye view of Jasmine's world!

♥ The city

In the market place, the merchant isn't pleased when Jasmine gives an apple to a hungry child without realizing she should pay for it!

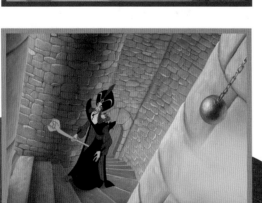

In the throne room, there is a hidden door that leads up to Jafar's secret lair. He goes there to think up ways to overthrow the Sultan.

The golden minarets glow in the sunlight.

Jafar's secret lair

The Sultan's palace is surrounded by beautiful, exotic gardens. But even in these gardens Jasmine feels trapped and wants to see the city that lies beyond the palace walls.

Aladdin's secret hideaway is on the rooftop of an old, abandoned building. He has amazing views of the whole city and can even see the Sultan's palace.

In the desert, on the outskirts of the city, the Cave of Wonders appears. The cave is filled with precious jewels and treasures. It is here that Aladdin finds the Magic Lamp.

The Sultan's palace

The dungeon is located underneath the palace. This is where Aladdin is held after he is arrested by Jafar's men.

Eastern magic

IT MAY NOT LOOK LIKE much on the outside, but when Aladdin rubs the dirty old lamp, an all-powerful Genie appears. The Genie can grant his new master three wishes and could make Aladdin as powerful as the Sultan. But all Aladdin wants is to marry Jasmine—and in the end he doesn't need magic or the Genie to make her love him.

It feels good to be out after all those years inside the lamp!

The Genie has phenomenal cosmic powers.

The Genie

The Genie feels a little cramped inside the tiny lamp, his home for the last 10,000 years.

The Genie understands Jasmine's longing for freedom. Like her, he wants to be able to make his own choices and be his own master. Although the Genie is powerful, he can only grant other people's wishes—not his own.

The Magic Carpet can fly faster than the wind!

Jasmine loves to see the world by air.

Iago is Jafar's noisy, bad-tempered parrot.

💙 The Magic Carpet

Stuck in the Cave of Wonders, Aladdin and Abu might never have escaped if it were not for the Magic Carpet. Although shy and timid at first, the Carpet becomes their friend and helps them escape from danger.

Aladdin's first wish is that he be turned into the wealthy Prince Ali. After Jafar has been defeated, Aladdin has his final wish. He asks that the Genie be set free from the lamp.

Jafar steals the Magic Lamp and the Genie is forced to obey his evil wishes. Aladdin knows that Jafar craves power, and cleverly tricks him into wishing to be a genie. Jafar's wish comes true and he becomes trapped in the lamp forever.

May all your wishes come true!

Mulan

A long, long time ago in Ancient China there lived a young girl named Mulan. She was a kind and loving daughter, but Mulan had an unfortunate habit of causing trouble without meaning to. She longed to find a path that would bring happiness and make her parents proud.

You don't meet a girl like that every dynasty.

A special girl

MULAN KNOWS THAT she will never be refined and graceful like the other girls, but she tries hard to please her family. She looks after her father, helps around the home by feeding the chickens, and tries not to cause too much trouble.

Loving family

Mulan's mother and grandmother think she should get married and take her to see a matchmaker. If the matchmaker likes Mulan she will help her make a good marriage.

ABOUT MULAN

♥ She's kind and caring, but also a little clumsy and accident prone!

♥ She loves her family more than anything and will do anything to make them happy.

♥ She's brave and clever.

Although Mulan is not happy to be meeting the matchmaker, she tries her best because she loves her family. She manages to look elegant, but soon spoils the pretty picture by dancing the wrong steps and then accidentally setting the matchmaker on fire!

Hair that just won't stay neat!

Belt to make her waist look tiny.

At home Mulan's best friends are a horse and dog, who look out for her and help her with the chores.

When Mulan starts her journey some new friends accompany her—Mushu the dragon and the lucky Cri-kee.

Family honor

Mulan longs to bring honor to her family but doesn't know how. When her father is called up to fight in the army, Mulan thinks he is too sick to make the trip.

Simple style of dress

It's going to take a miracle to get into the army.

In the middle of the night, Mulan steals her father's armor and sword so that she can take his place in the army. She disguises herself as a boy named Ping and sets off on a crazy adventure.

Finding herself

MULAN WANTS TO SAVE her father but joining the army is no picnic, nor is pretending to be a smelly man! But Mulan is determined to succeed and bring honor to her family. Although she has Mushu and Cri-kee by her side, her fellow new recruits don't seem very friendly.

Dangerous times

China is under threat from the invading Huns so the Emperor calls up every available male into the army. The Emperor is a wise and great man but his advisor Chi Fu is not so smart.

At first Mulan's fellow soldiers don't seem to like "Ping" very much, but "his" courage and strength win them over. Eventually!

The soldiers are led by Captain Li Shang. He is tough and brave and wants his men to be just like him.

Mulan has to prove to Shang that "Ping" has what it takes to be a good soldier. Through hard work and perseverance she shows him she can do it.

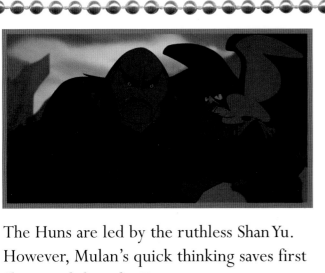

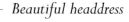
Beautiful headdress

The Huns are led by the ruthless Shan Yu. However, Mulan's quick thinking saves first Shang and then the Emperor.

The Emperor is proud of Mulan and honors her with a medal and a sword.

Mulan is able to return home with honor and pride. Her father is just happy to see her!

Ornate, jewel-encrusted sleeves

Beautifully patterned garment worn over dress

Simple dress underneath

Happy at last

Mulan has found both happiness and honor and she is delighted to be home. After some wise words from the Emperor, Shang goes to see Mulan—and even her grandmother approves of him!

Pocahontas

Many years ago in what was then known by many people as the New World, a free-spirited girl longed for adventure. Her name was Pocahontas and her dreams seemed to be telling her that something amazing would happen to her soon, but her father wanted her to settle down and get married.

This is the path I choose.

Free spirit

Long dark hair that blows in the wind

POCAHONTAS IS A MEMBER of the Powhatan tribe. She loves roaming the beautiful lands around her village and dreams of great adventures just around the corner. Her father is the Chief and he thinks his carefree daughter should settle down and marry the tribe's bravest warrior, Kocoum.

This necklace belonged to Pocahontas' mother

 ## Family ties

Pocahontas' father is an important man. He must take care of the whole tribe and make difficult decisions.

When Pocahontas needs advice, she visits Grandmother Willow. The ancient talking tree is extremely wise.

Simple dress made of animal skins

The Powhatan tribe care for and respect the land they live on. They will do anything they can to keep it safe.

Pocahontas does not need shoes

Pocahontas' best friends

Nakoma is Pocahontas' very best friend.

Meeko and Flit look out for Pocahontas.

Although Pocahontas is a free spirit she has some special friends, including a racoon named Meeko and tiny bird named Flit.

Kocoum is a handsome warrior, but also very serious.

Flit is always hungry!

ABOUT POCAHONTAS

♥ Stubborn and independent, she doesn't want to marry Kocoum.

♥ Pocahontas means "little mischief".

♥ She is also brave enough to stand up for what she believes in.

It seems that Pocahontas is right, an amazing change is coming. English adventurer Captain John Smith is sailing to the New World to find gold and other riches. But he may not find a warm welcome from the Powhatan tribe.

John Smith finds something more valuable than gold when he meets Pocahontas—true love!

Against the odds

AT FIRST POCAHONTAS and John Smith do not trust each other. By listening to their hearts they soon begin to understand each other better and it is not long before they realize that they are falling in love. But they know they must keep their feelings hidden from their friends and families.

 Greedy visitor

John Smith is working for Governor Ratcliffe, a greedy man who just wants wealth and power. He believes that Pocahontas and her tribe are hiding lots of valuable gold.

John Smith and Pocahontas are not the only ones who are making new friends. When Meeko meets Governor Ratcliffe's pampered pet dog, Percy, the unlikely pair become pals!

When Pocahontas and John Smith's romance becomes public, it very nearly leads to tragedy. First Pocahontas saves John Smith's life, then John saves her father from the Governor's bullet.

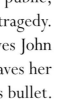

Tough goodbye

John Smith takes the bullet meant for the Chief and very nearly loses his own life. He must return home if he is to survive.

Long hair arranged in elegant "up" do

Pocahontas bids farewell to John Smith, knowing they will never forget each other.

Elegant lace cuffs

Pretty gold bows

Beautiful full skirt

DK

LONDON, NEW YORK, MELBOURNE,
MUNICH, AND DELHI

DESIGNER *Cathy Tincknell*
BRAND MANAGER AND SENIOR DESIGNER *Lisa Lanzarini*
SENIOR EDITORS *Lindsay Kent and Catherine Saunders*
WRITTEN BY *Naia Bray-Moffatt and Catherine Saunders*
ART DIRECTOR *Mark Richards*
PUBLISHING MANAGERS *Cynthia O'Neill Collins and Simon Beecroft*
PRODUCTION EDITORS *Eric Shapland and Clare Mclean*
CATEGORY PUBLISHER *Alex Allan*
PRODUCTION CONTROLLERS *Nicola Torode and Nick Seston*
ADDITIONAL ART *Marco Colletti, Silvano Scolari and Vincenzo Genna*
JACKET DESIGN *Lisa Lanzarini*

First Canadian Paperback Edition, 2008
08 09 10 9 8 7 6 5 4 3 2

First published in 2003
Dorling Kindersley is represented in Canada by
Tourmaline Editions Inc., 662 King Street West, Suite 304
Toronto, Ontario M5V 1M7

ISBN 978-1-55363-095-1

Color reproduction by MDP, UK
Printed and bound at Toppan, China.

Discover more at
www.dk.com